SCHOLASTIC
Learning Express

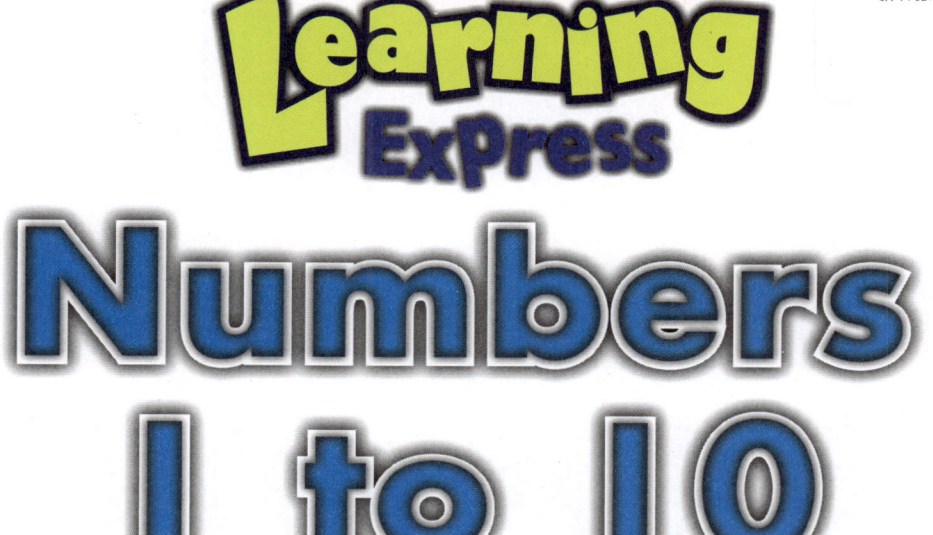

Numbers 1 to 10

This book belongs to

_____

Copyright © 2005, 2010 by Scholastic Inc.
Copyright © 2012 by Scholastic Education International (Singapore) Private Limited
All rights reserved.

Previously published as Reading & Math Jumbo Workbook PreK and Summer Express PreK-K
by Scholastic Inc.

This edition published by Scholastic Education International (Singapore) Private Limited
A division of Scholastic Inc.

No part of this publication may be reproduced in whole or in part, or stored in a retrieval
system, or transmitted in any form or by any means, electronic, mechanical, photocopying,
recording, or otherwise without the written permission of the publisher. For information
regarding permission, write to:
Scholastic Education International (Singapore) Private Limited
81 Ubi Avenue 4 #02-28 UB.ONE Singapore 408830
education@scholastic.com.sg

First edition 2012
Reprinted 2012

ISBN 978-981-07-1351-5

Welcome to Scholastic Learning Express!

Helping your child build essential skills is easy!
These teacher-approved activities have been specially developed to make learning both accessible and enjoyable. On each page, you'll find:

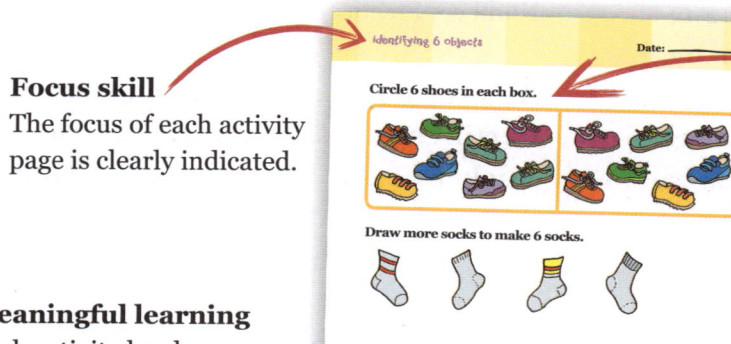

Focus skill
The focus of each activity page is clearly indicated.

Instructions
The read-aloud instructions are easy for your child to understand.

Meaningful learning
Each activity has been carefully designed to make your child's learning meaningful and fun.

This book also contains:

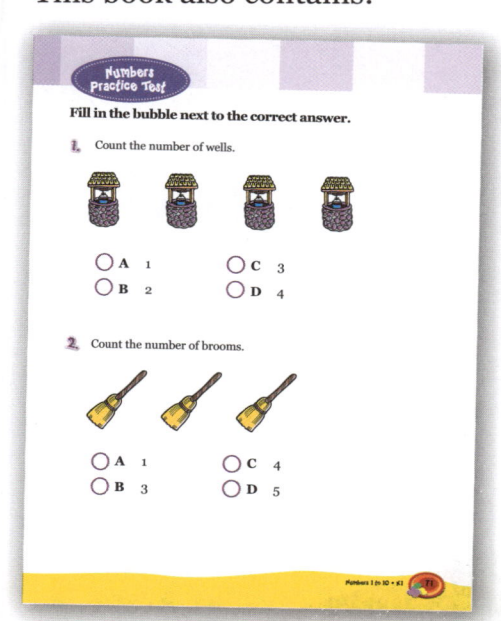

Instant assessment to ensure your child really masters the skills.

Completion certificate to celebrate your child's leap in learning.

Motivational stickers to mark the milestones of your child's learning path.

Contents

Numbers 1 to 10.......................... 5
identifying and writing number 1 6-8
identifying and writing number 2 9-11
identifying and writing number 3 12-14
identifying and writing number 4 15-17
identifying and writing number 5 18-20
identifying and writing number 6 21-23
identifying and writing number 7 24-26
identifying and writing number 8 27-29
identifying and writing number 9 30-32
identifying and writing number 10 33-35
identifying number words 1 to 10 36
identifying numbers 1 to 10.................. 37
counting 38-40
identifying 1 object 41
identifying 2 objects 42
identifying 3 objects 43
identifying 1 to 3 objects 44
identifying 4 objects 45
identifying 5 objects 46
identifying 1 to 5 objects....................... 47-48
identifying 6 objects 49
identifying 7 objects 50
identifying 8 objects 51
identifying 9 objects 52
identifying 10 objects 53
counting groups of 1 to 10 objects........ 54
counting groups of 2 to 10 objects 55
ordering numbers from 1 to 10 56-60
identifying equal groups....................... 61-62

forming equal groups 63-64
counting more than 65-67
counting less than................................. 68-70
Numbers Practice Test 71-76

Answer Key 77
Certificate... 79
Stickers... 81-85

Numbers 1 to 10

Recognizing and writing numerals, counting and counting by groups ("skip-counting") are crucial to children's early mathematics learning. In addition, concepts, such as "more than," "less than," "equal" and identifying quantities of items, are all key to success in mathematics.

What to Do
Read the directions on each page to your child. When finished, help your child check the work. Offer lots of praise for being such a "marvelous mathematician!"

Keep on Going!
Count everything around you — wheels on a car, stripes on a shirt, sections of an orange!

identifying and writing number 1   Date: _____

Number Practice

Trace the number.

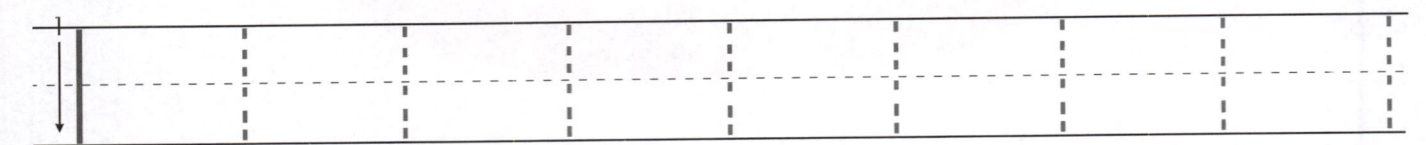

Write the number.

Trace the word.

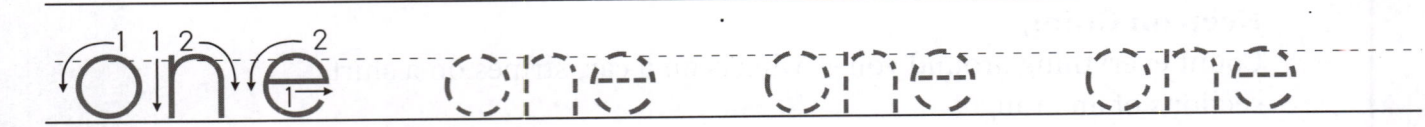

one   one   one   one

Write the word.

Number Hunt

Circle every number 1.

6	3	1	8	9	2	8	3	2	1	2
2	2	4	6	1	5	9	1	5	6	3
5	9	6	7	8	1	7	8	3	4	1
1	3	8	1	9	7	4	7	9	3	1

identifying and writing number 1

Date: _____

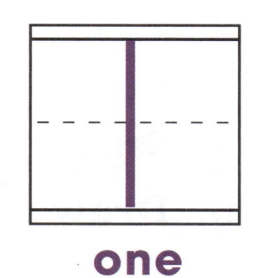

one

1. **Paste** 1 ☀ in the sky.

2. **Paste** 1 🐦 in the sky.

3. **Paste** 1 ✈ in the sky.

identifying and writing number 1   Date: _____

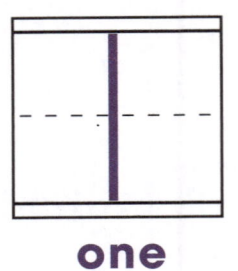

one

1. **Draw** 1 🌈 in the sky.

2. **Draw** 1 🪁 in the sky.

3. **Draw** 1 🎈 in the sky.

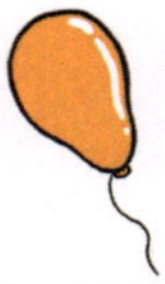

identifying and writing number 2

Date: _____

Number Practice

Trace the number.

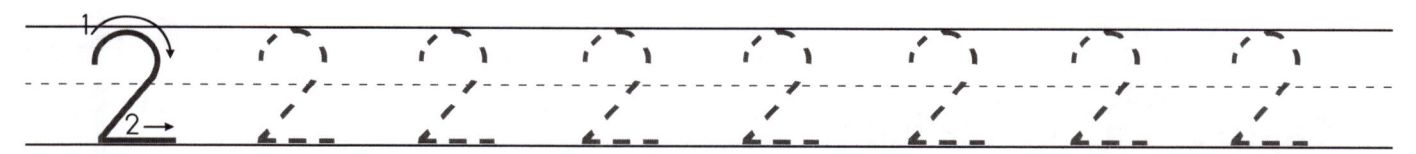

2 2 2 2 2 2 2 2

Write the number.

Trace the word.

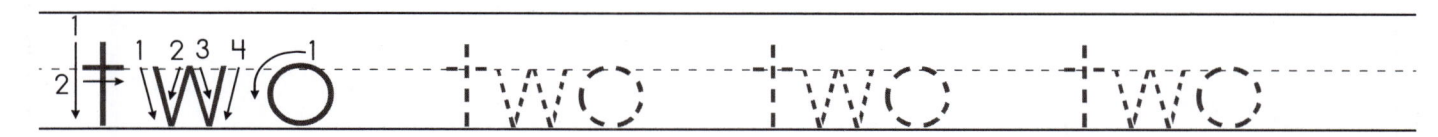

two two two two

Write the word.

Number Hunt

Circle every number 2.

3	10	4	6	9	2	3	2	5	7
2	9	3	1	4	2	9	5	6	5
7	3	2	6	6	8	1	7	9	2
9	2	1	9	5	4	2	8	1	6

Numbers 1 to 10 • K1   9

identifying and writing number 2   Date: _____

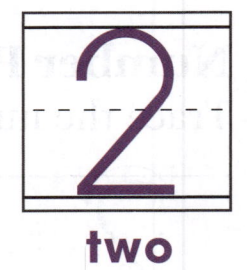

2
two

1. **Paste** 2 🌳 on the hill.

2. **Paste** 2 🐐 on the hill.

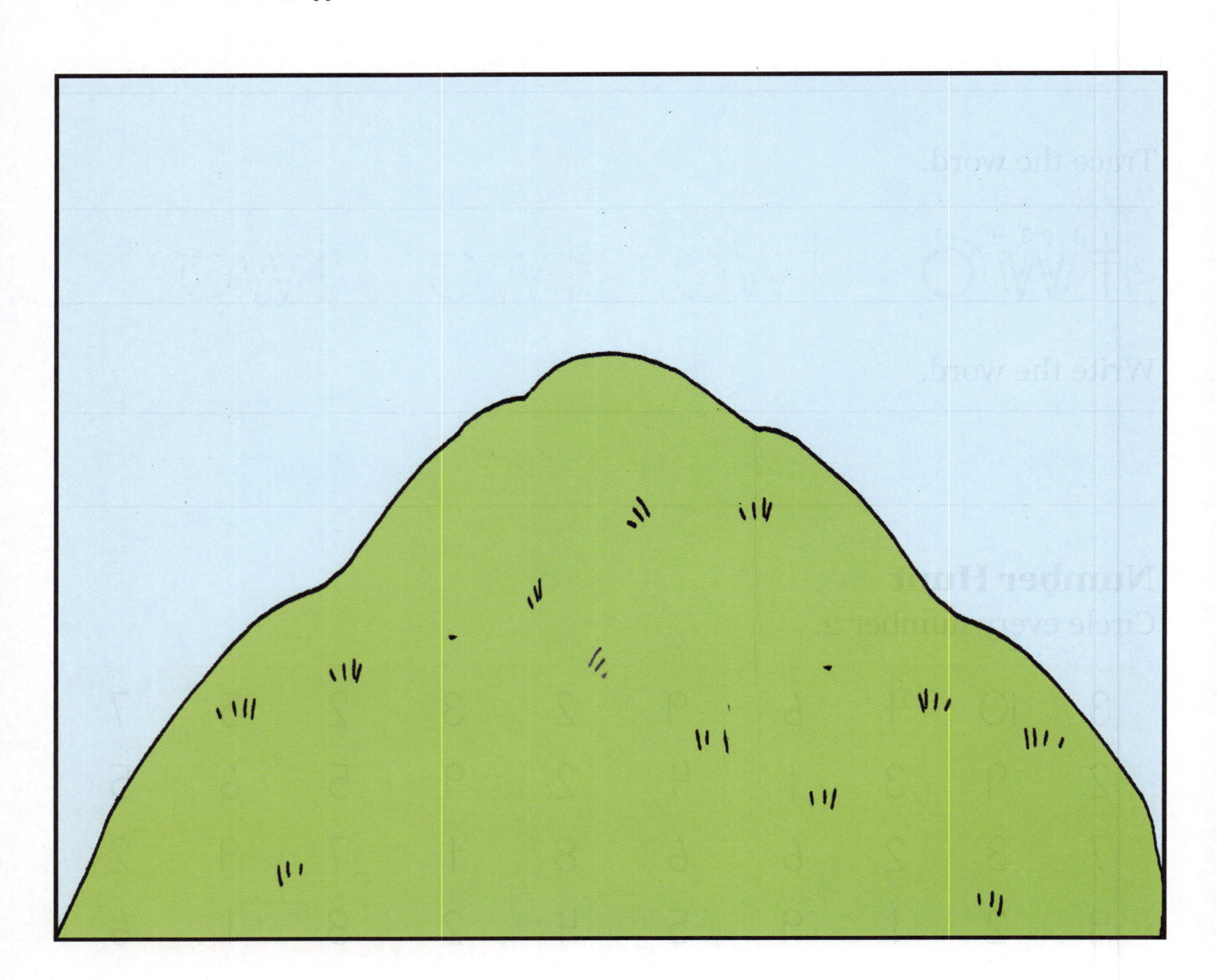

10 Numbers 1 to 10 • K1

identifying and writing number 2

Date: _____

2
two

1. **Draw** 2 🥚 in the nest.

2. **Draw** 2 🐦 in the nest.

Numbers 1 to 10 • K1   11

identifying and writing number 3

Date: _____

Number Practice

Trace the number.

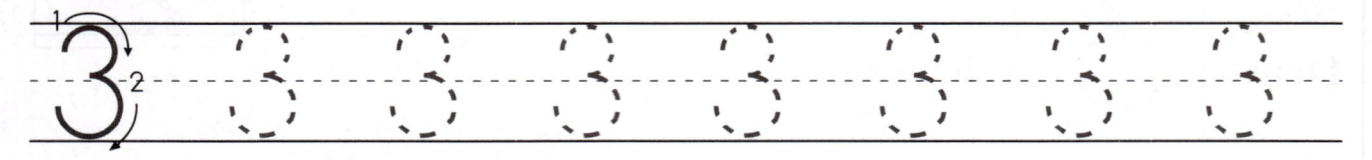

3 3 3 3 3 3 3 3

Write the number.

Trace the word.

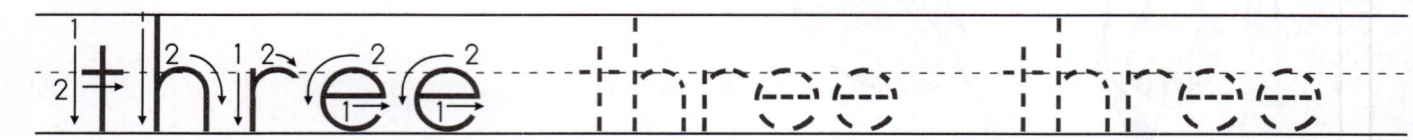

three three three

Write the word.

Number Hunt

Circle every number 3.

5	3	1	8	3	9	5	2	4	6
2	5	7	2	3	2	3	9	8	1
8	6	4	3	1	5	4	3	2	8
3	8	9	1	3	7	9	8	1	10

identifying and writing number 3

Date: _____

3
three

1. **Paste** 3 [fish] in the bowl.

2. **Paste** 3 [fish] in the bowl.

Numbers 1 to 10 • K1   13

identifying and writing number 3

Date: _____

1. **Draw** 3 🐳 in the ocean.

3
three

identifying and writing number 4

Date: _____

Number Practice

Trace the number.

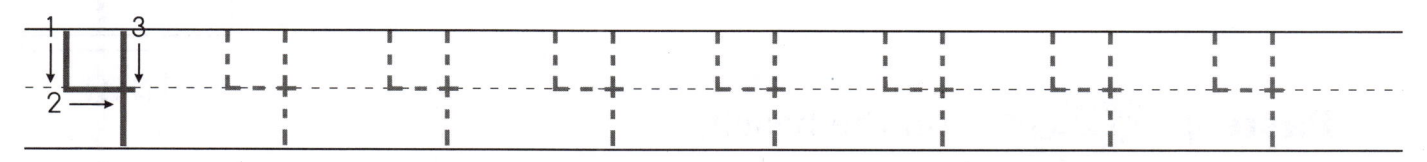

4 4 4 4 4 4 4 4 4 4

Write the number.

Trace the word.

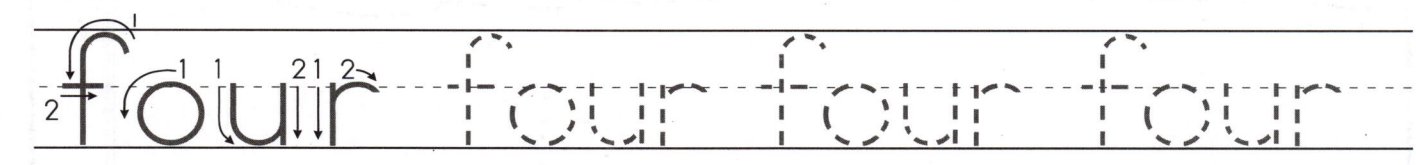

four four four four

Write the word.

Number Hunt

Circle every number 4.

3	6	5	4	6	3	8	5	9	7	9
1	1	2	1	5	10	4	6	9	6	2
5	8	2	4	1	5	8	4	9	5	1
7	6	4	6	3	7	2	7	8	9	2

Numbers 1 to 10 • K1   15

identifying and writing number 4

Date: _____

4

four

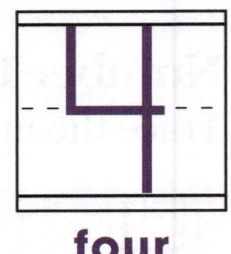

1. **Paste** 4 🦀 on the beach.

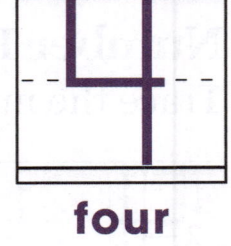

2. **Paste** 4 🐚 on the beach.

identifying and writing number 4

Date: _____

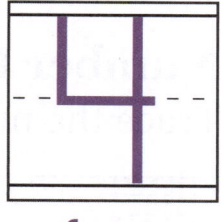

1. **Draw** 4 ● on the T-shirt.

2. **Draw** 4 ▲ on the T-shirt.

four

Numbers 1 to 10 • K1

identifying and writing number 5 Date: _____

Number Practice
Trace the number.

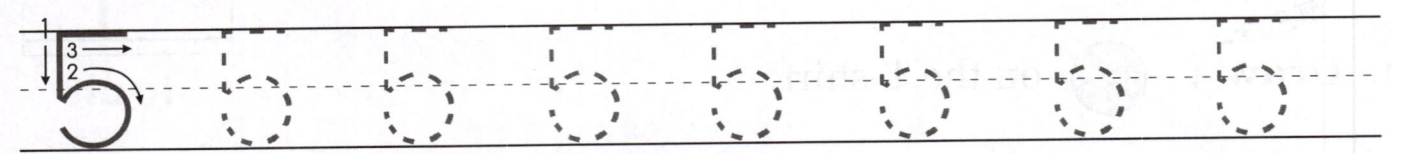

5 5 5 5 5 5 5 5

Write the number.

Trace the word.

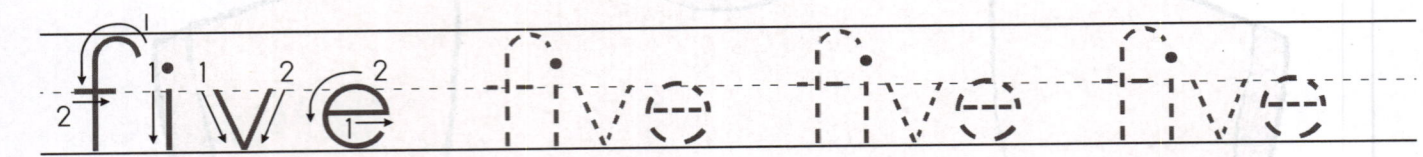

five five five five

Write the word.

Number Hunt
Circle every number 5.

2	5	3	10	1	4	5	8	9	6	10
6	4	8	5	2	1	7	5	6	9	5
7	3	8	1	9	5	6	7	5	1	4
1	4	5	9	2	3	9	2	1	10	8

18 Numbers 1 to 10 • K1

identifying and writing number 5

Date: _____

5
five

1. **Paste** 5 🐞 on the leaf.

Numbers 1 to 10 • K1   19

identifying and writing number 5

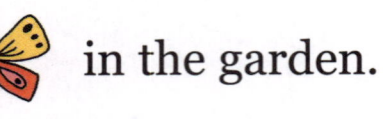

Date: _____

5
five

1. Draw 5 🦋 in the garden.

identifying and writing number 6

Date: _____

Number Practice

Trace the number.

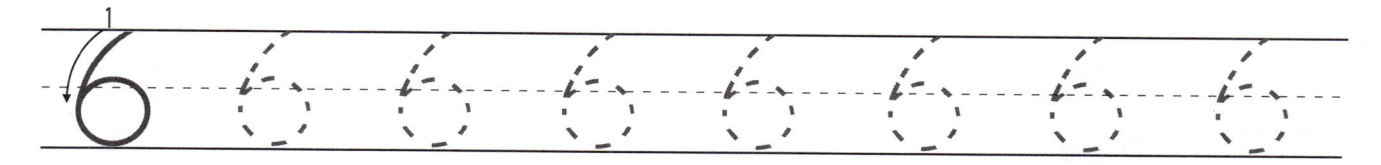

6 6 6 6 6 6 6 6

Write the number.

Trace the word.

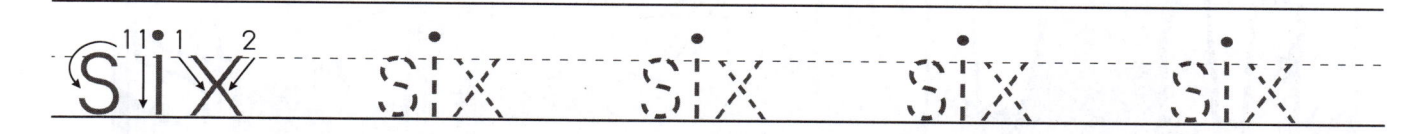

six six six six six

Write the word.

Number Hunt

Circle every number 6.

10	2	1	8	3	9	6	2	6	2	5
8	6	7	2	9	5	3	6	8	1	9
6	7	2	6	3	10	5	6	3	2	6
6	9	1	3	7	9	8	10	1	6	8

identifying and writing number 6

Date: _____

6
six

1. **Paste** 6 on the forest floor.

identifying and writing number 6

Date: _____

1. **Draw** 6 🍄 near the log.

six

identifying and writing number 7   Date: _____

Number Practice
Trace the number.

7 7 7 7 7 7 7 7

Write the number.

Trace the word.

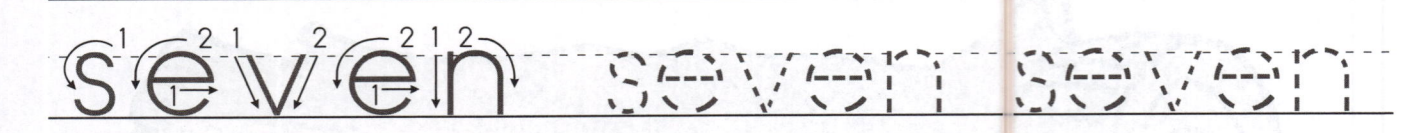

seven seven seven

Write the word.

Number Hunt
Circle every number 7.

5	7	1	8	3	9	5	7	4	6
1	5	7	6	3	2	3	9	8	1
2	6	4	3	7	5	4	3	2	10
8	7	9	1	3	7	9	8	10	4

24 Numbers 1 to 10 • K1

identifying and writing number 7

Date: _____

7
seven

1. **Paste** 7 🍭 in the candy jar.

identifying and writing number 7 Date: _____

7
seven

1. **Draw 7** 🕯️ on the cake.

26 Numbers 1 to 10 • K1

identifying and writing number 8

Date: _____

Number Practice
Trace the number.

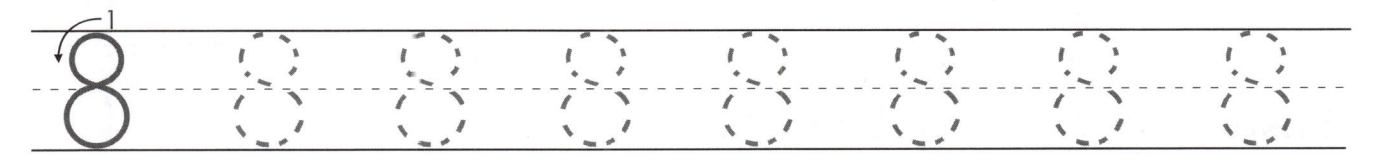

8 8 8 8 8 8 8 8

Write the number.

Trace the word.

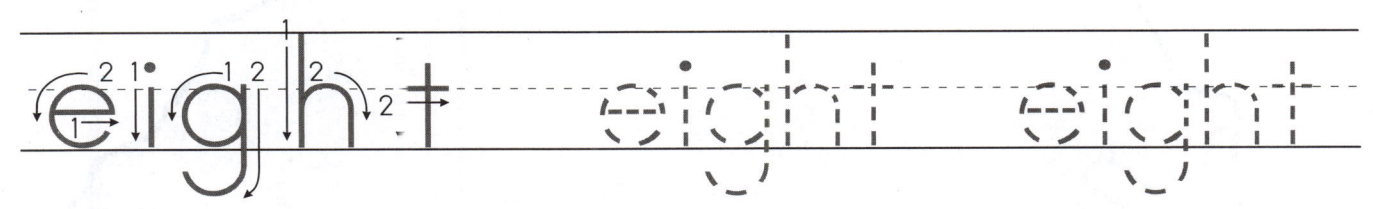

eight eight eight

Write the word.

Number Hunt
Circle every number 8.

9	5	2	4	6	8	3	4	10	8
2	3	6	3	9	2	5	7	8	1
4	8	10	5	4	3	2	10	5	8
1	8	7	9	8	10	4	9	3	10

Numbers 1 to 10 • K1   27

identifying and writing number 8

Date: _____

8
eight

1. **Paste** 8 🦎 on the rock.

identifying and writing number 8

Date: _____

8
eight

1. **Draw** 8 🕷 on the web.

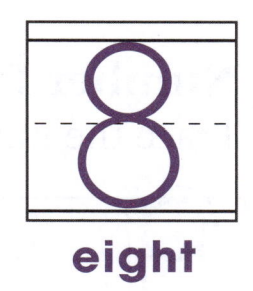

Numbers 1 to 10 • K1   29

identifying and writing number 9

Date: _____

Number Practice

Trace the number.

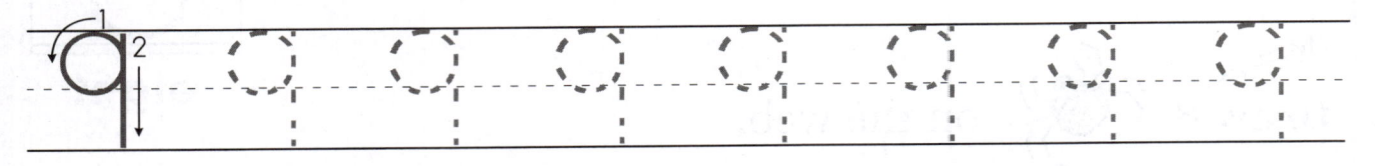

9 9 9 9 9 9 9 9

Write the number.

Trace the word.

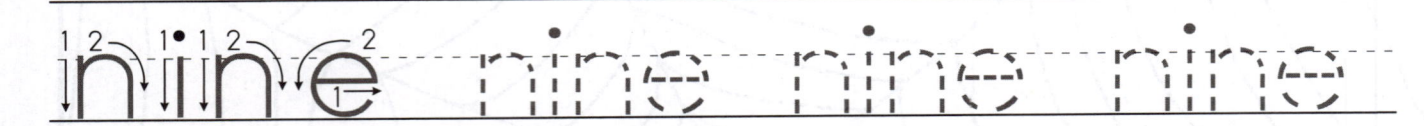

nine nine nine nine

Write the word.

Number Hunt

Circle every number 9.

9	3	1	8	3	9	5	2	4	6
8	1	2	2	5	7	2	3	5	3
10	9	4	3	2	8	9	8	6	4
9	7	2	8	10	3	10	2	9	5

identifying and writing number 9

Date: _____

q
nine

1. **Paste** 9 in the field.

identifying and writing number 9

Date: ———————

q

nine

1. **Draw** 9 ⭐ in the sky.

identifying and writing number 10

Date: _____

Number Practice

Trace the number.

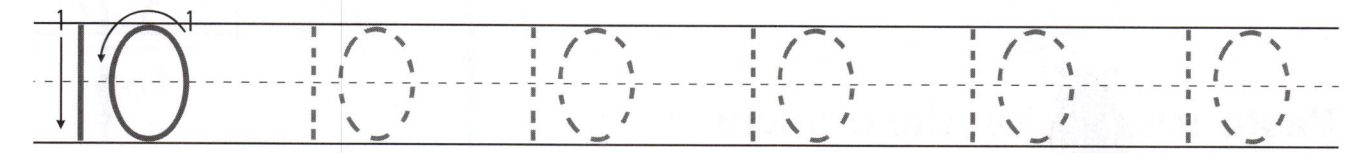

10 10 10 10 10 10 10

Write the number.

Trace the word.

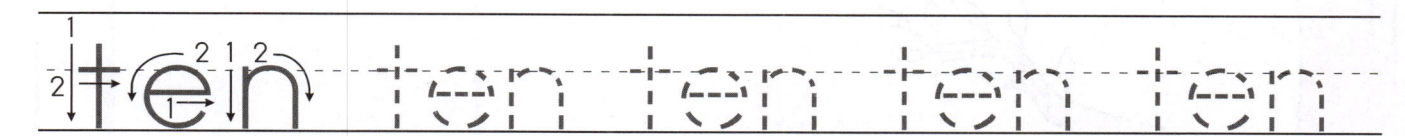

ten ten ten ten ten

Write the word.

Number Hunt

Circle every number 10.

2	4	6	10	3	1	8	10	9	2
10	5	3	9	8	1	2	6	5	7
3	9	5	4	3	10	7	5	8	10
7	10	8	10	1	9	3	10	9	1

Numbers 1 to 10 • K1   33

identifying and writing number 10

Date: _____

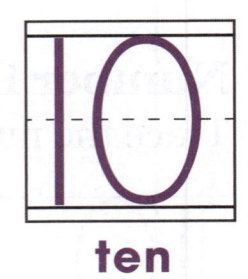

10
ten

1. **Paste** 10 🦉 on the branches.

34 Numbers 1 to 10 • K1

identifying and writing number 10

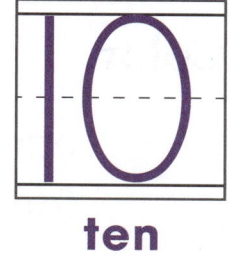

Date: _____

10
ten

1. **Draw** 10 🦇 in the cave.

Numbers 1 to 10 • K1   35

identifying number words 1 to 10

Date: _____

Color.

one = yellow
four = white
seven = red
ten = pink

two = black
five = orange
eight = purple

three = blue
six = green
nine = brown

identifying numbers 1 to 10

Date: _____

Color.

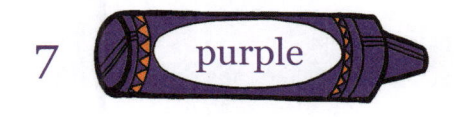

1 yellow
2 green
3 blue
4 black
5 red
6 brown
7 purple
8 orange

Numbers 1 to 10 • K1

counting

Date: _____

1. **Count** each kind of animal.

2. **Write** the number in the box.

counting

Date: _____

1. **Count** each kind of block.

2. **Write** the number in the box.

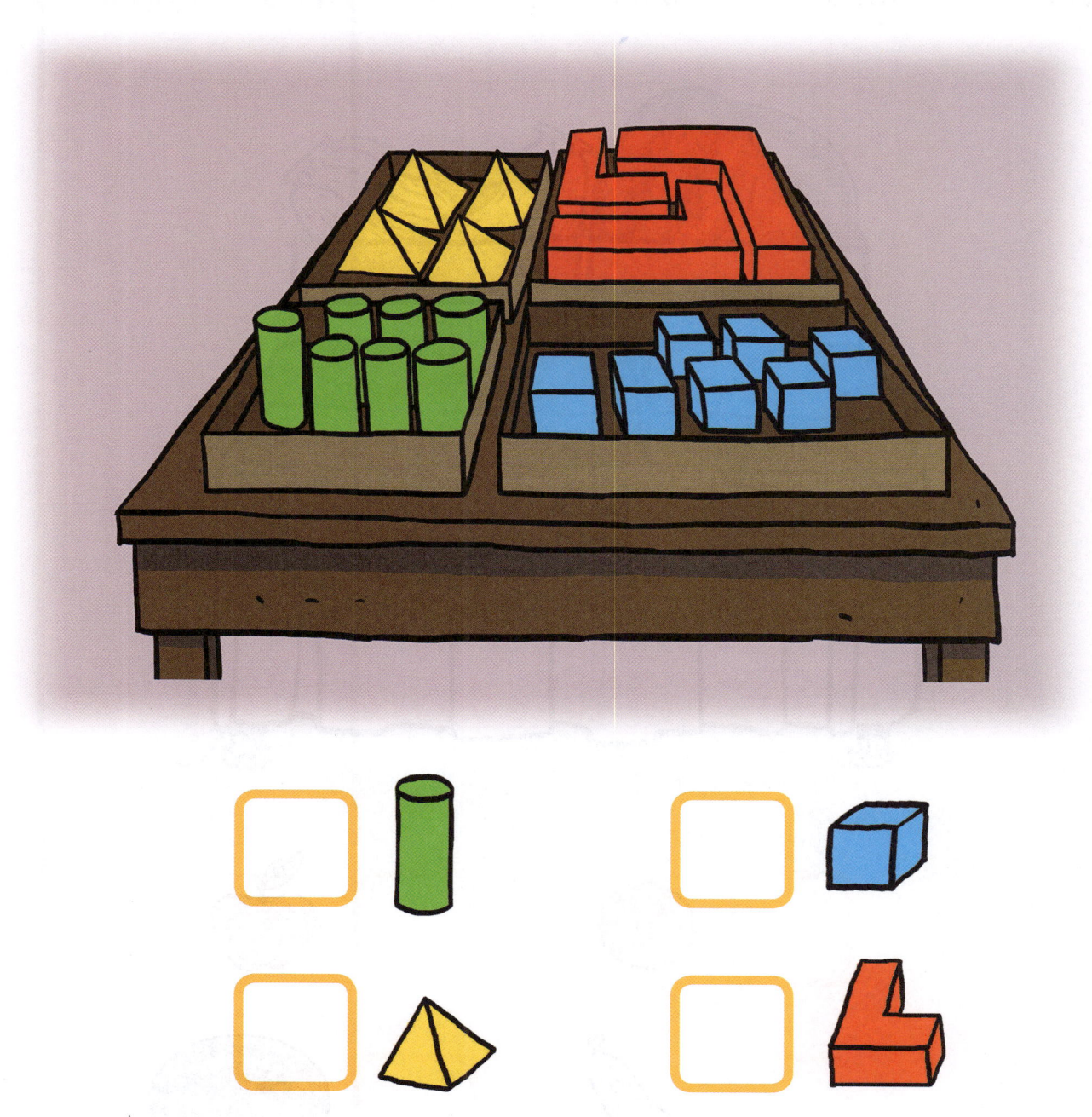

Numbers 1 to 10 • K1   39

counting

Date: _____

1. **Color** each kind of fruit.

2. **Write** the number in the box.

identifying 1 object

Date: _____

Color each shape with 1 fish.

Numbers 1 to 10 • K1   41

identifying 2 objects

Date: _____

Color each circle with 2 dots.

identifying 3 objects

Date: _____

Color each barge with 3 objects.

Draw 3 ▭ on each barge.

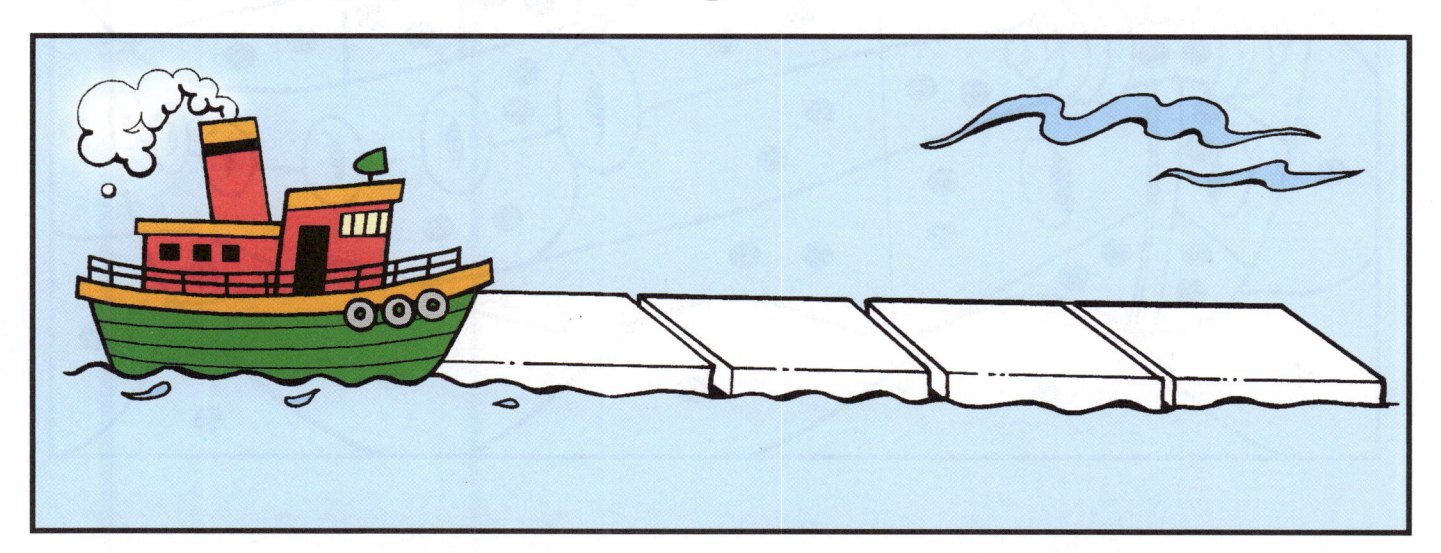

Numbers 1 to 10 • K1   43

identifying 1 to 3 objects

Date: _____

Color.

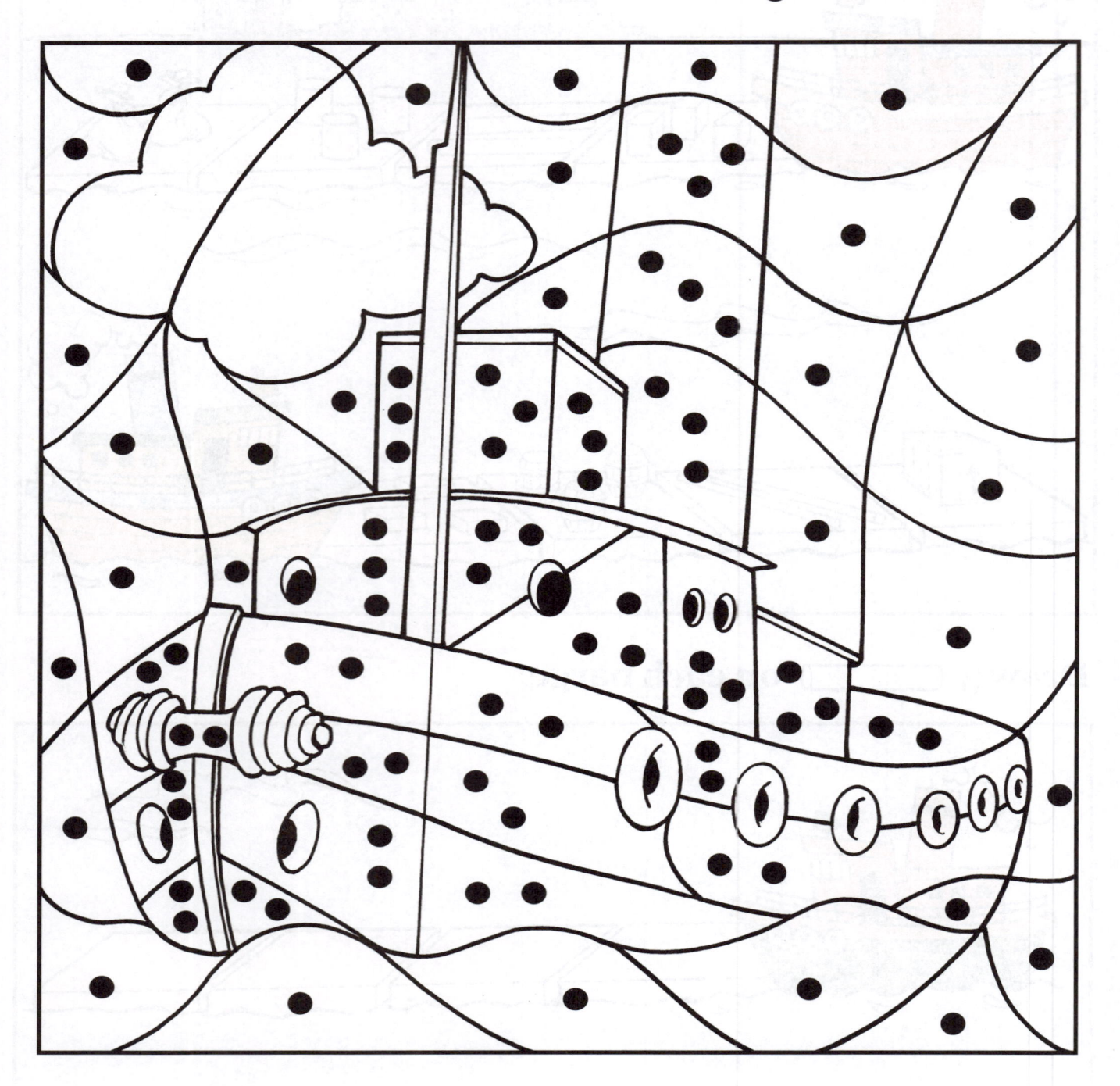

• = blue   : = brown   ∴ = red

identifying 4 objects

Date: _____

Color each dog with 4 spots.

Numbers 1 to 10 • K1

identifying 5 objects

Date: _____

Color each lily pad with 5 flies.

identifying 1 to 5 objects

Date: _____

Draw a line to match each number to the set of shapes.

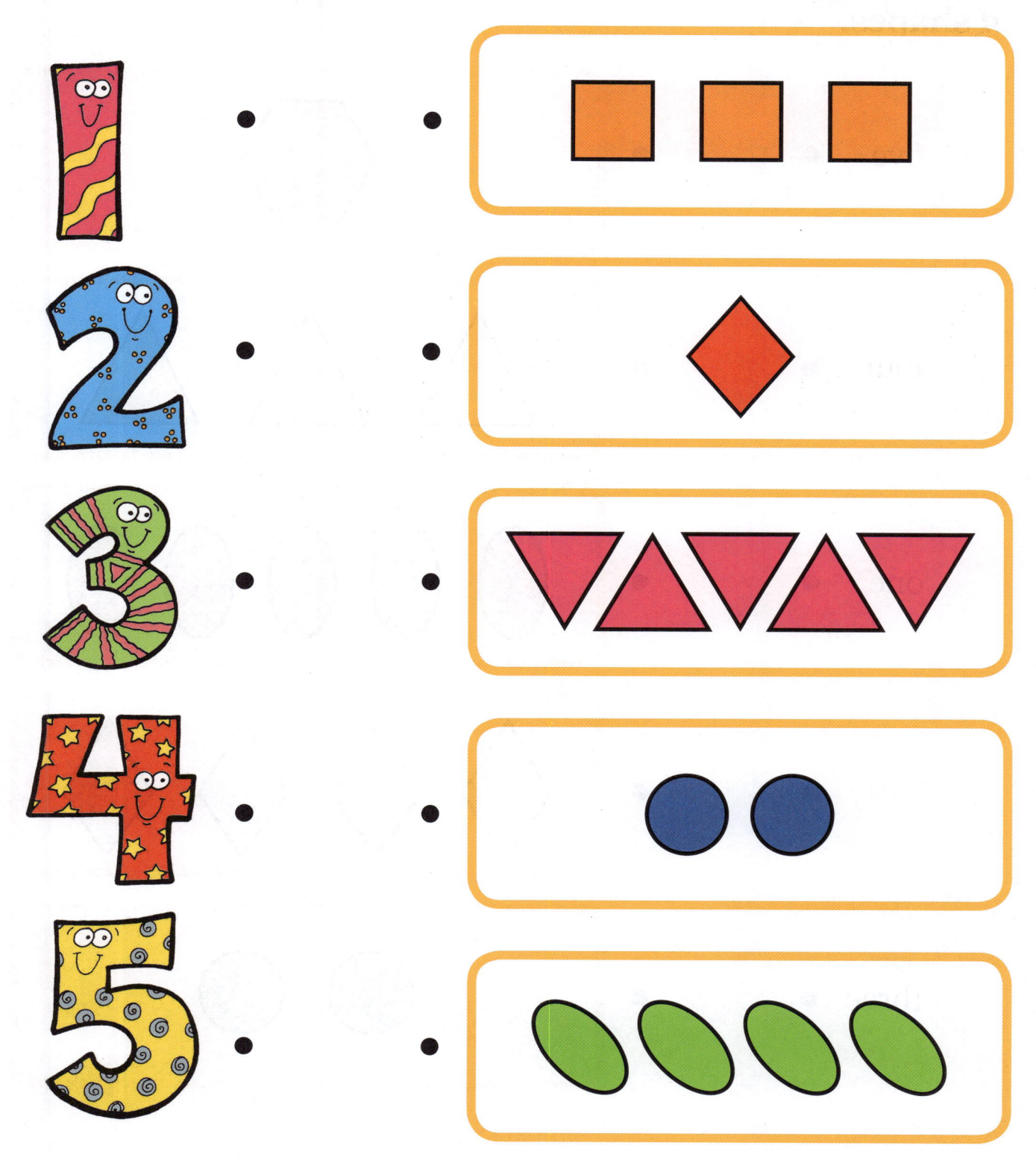

Numbers 1 to 10 • K1   47

identifying 1 to 5 objects

Date: _____

Draw a line to match each number word to the set of shapes.

five

four

one

two

three

identifying 6 objects

Date: _____

Circle 6 shoes in each box.

Draw more socks to make 6 socks.

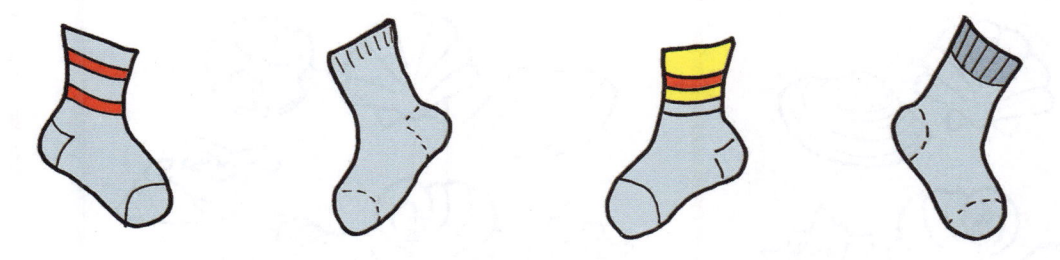

Count the socks. Write the correct number.

Numbers 1 to 10 • K1   49

identifying 7 objects

Date: _____

Color 7 shells in each box.

identifying 8 objects

Date: _____

Count the eels. Color the animal with the matching number.

Draw more eels in each box to make 8 eels.

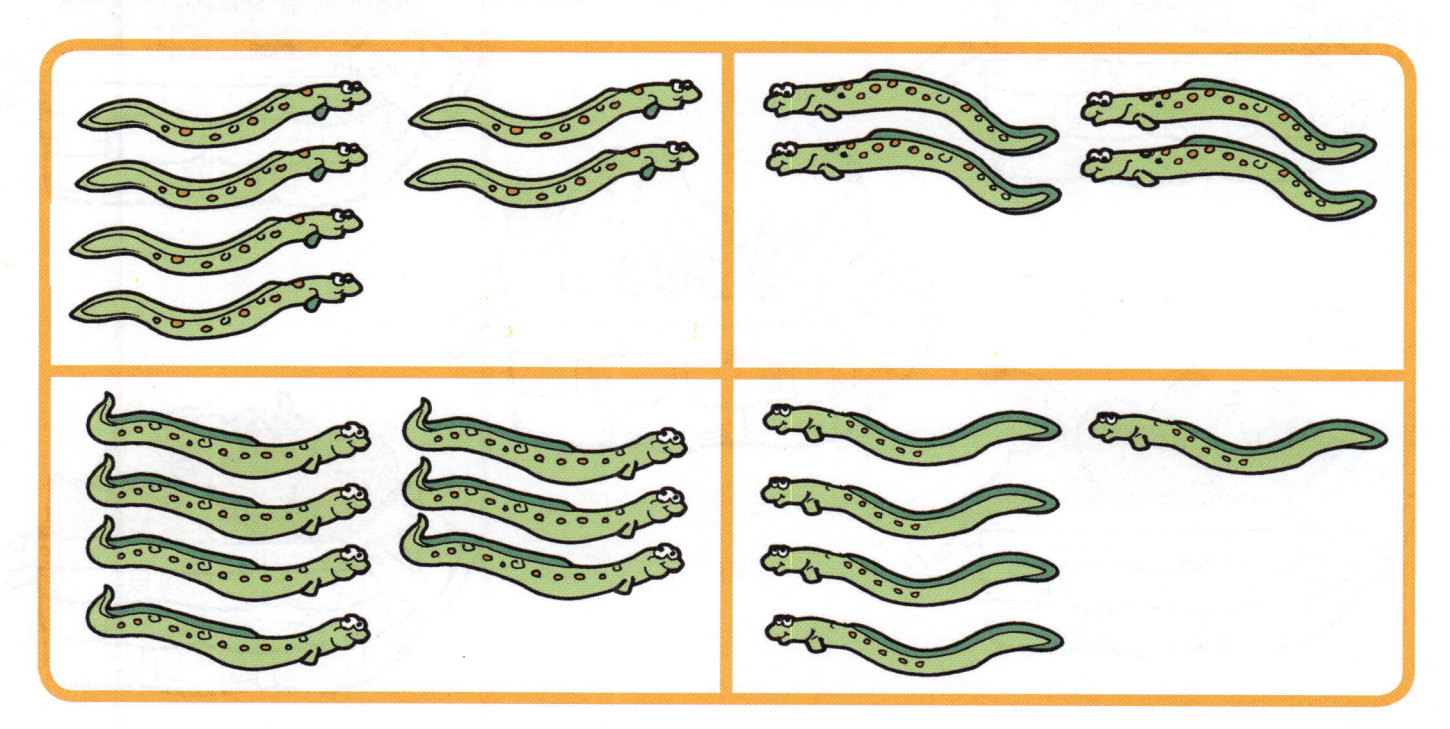

identifying 9 objects   Date: _____

Color each basket with 9 pieces of fruit.

identifying 10 objects

Date: _____

Help the train find the right track. Count each railroad tie. Color the track with 10 railroad ties red.

counting groups of 1 to 10 objects

Date: _____

Circle the correct number of objects.

1	
6	
10	
5	
2	
3	

counting groups of 2 to 10 objects

Date: _____

Color.

- = blue
- = red
- = green
- = orange
- = purple
- = black
- = brown
- = white
- = yellow

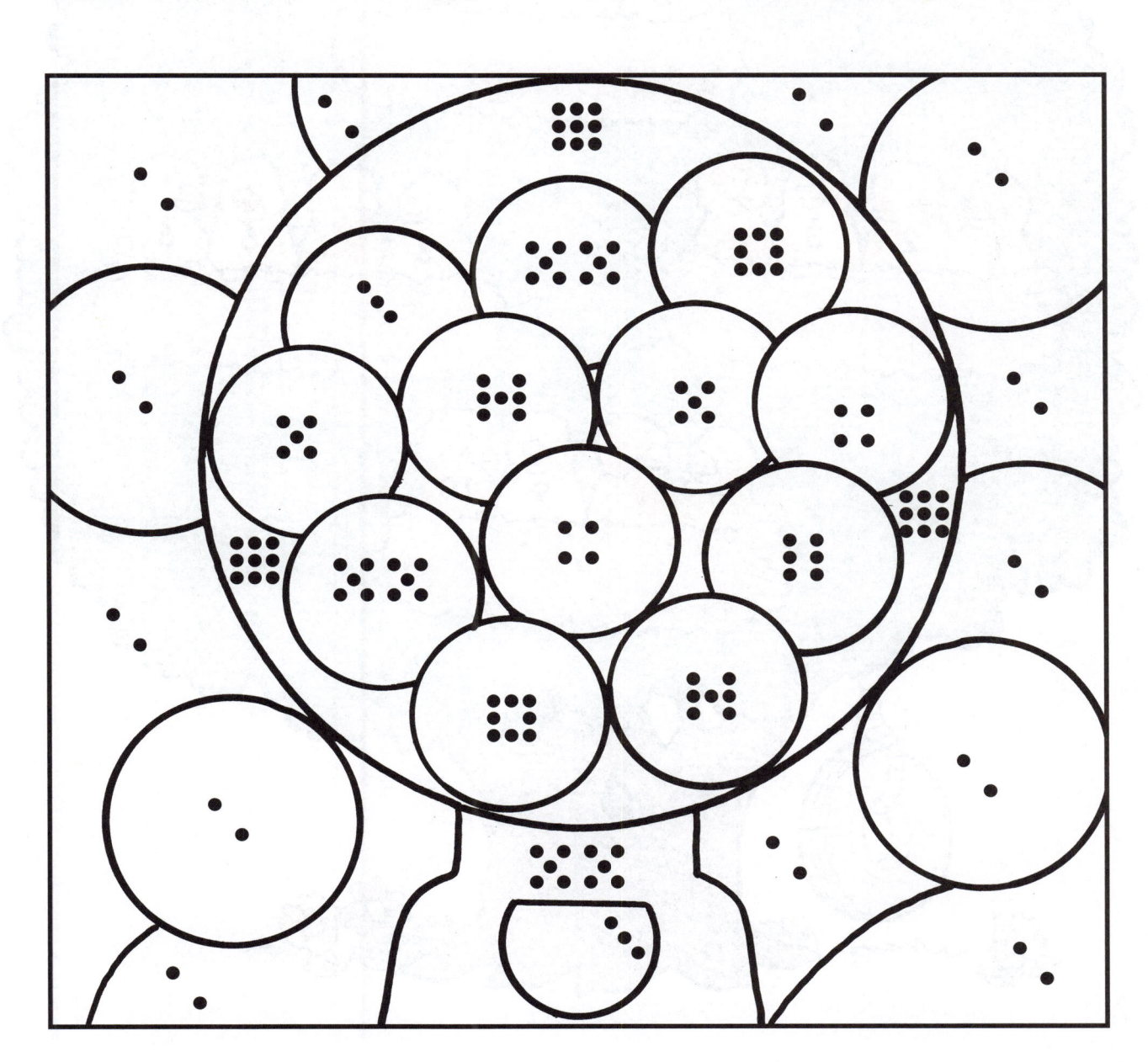

ordering numbers from 1 to 10

Date: _____

Write each missing number.

Nest 1: 5, 6, _, 8
Nest 2: 1, 2, 3, _
Nest 3: 3, _, 5, 6
Nest 4: 7, _, 9, 10

ordering numbers from 1 to 10

Date: _____

Write the missing numbers.

Join the dots from 1 to 10.

ordering numbers from 1 to 10

Date: _____

Join the dots from 1 to 10. Color.

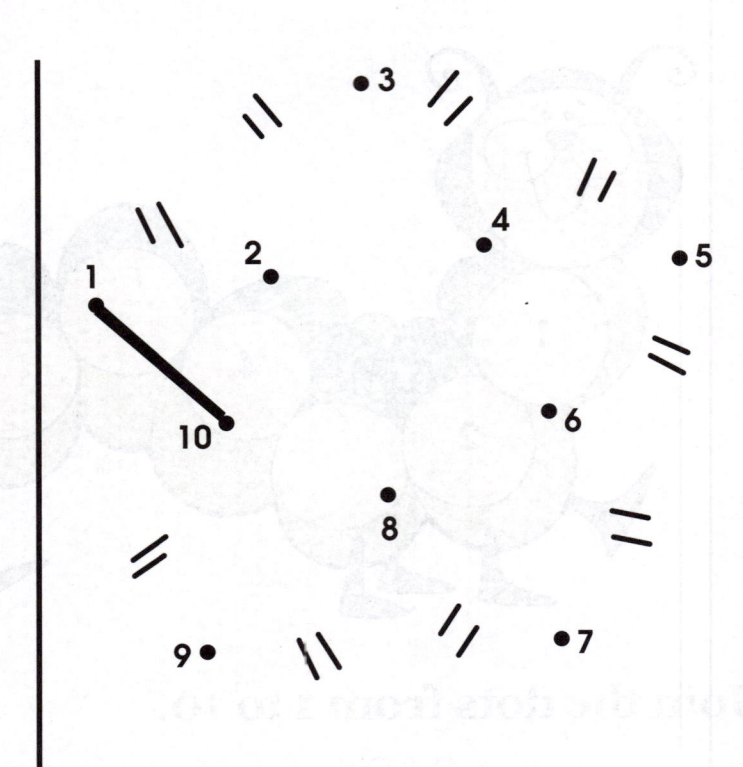

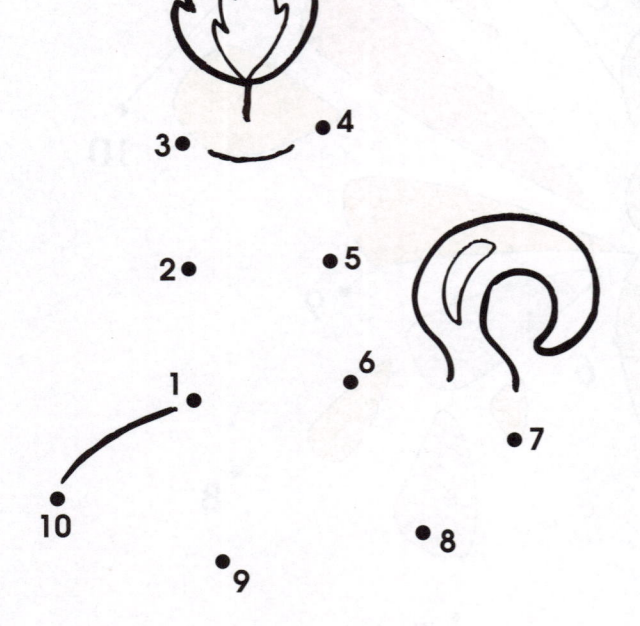

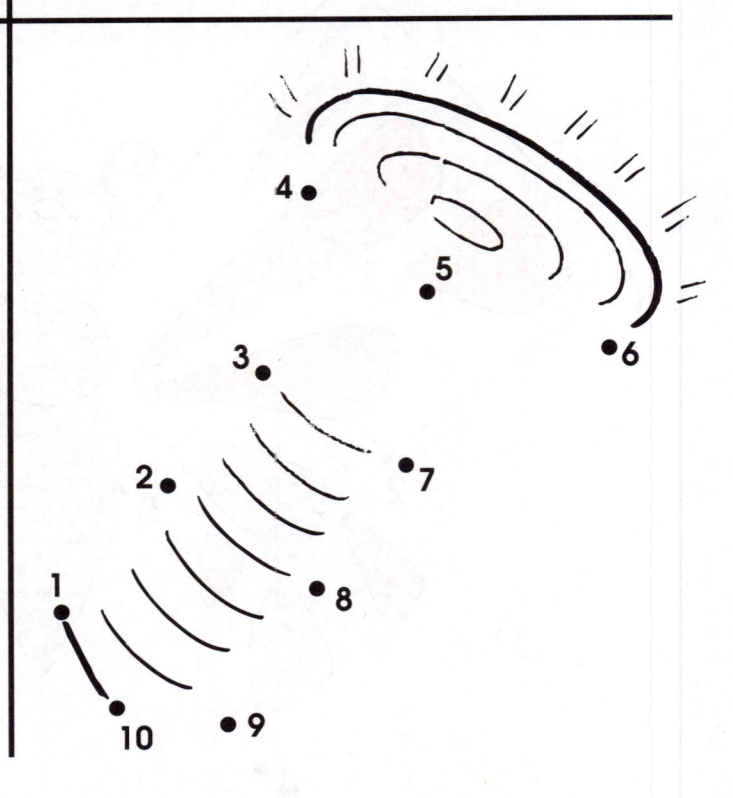

ordering numbers from 1 to 10

Date: _____

**Help the postman find his way to the post office.
Color the spaces from 1 to 10 in the correct order.**

	1	5	9	8	1
4	2	3	8	4	3
8	7	4	5	6	9
5	9	10	3	7	4
4	2	6	9	8	1
3	8	4	10	3	7
10	1	7			
9	5	3			

Numbers 1 to 10 • K1

ordering numbers from 1 to 10

Date: _____

Help the earthworm reach its home. Trace the path by following the correct order from 1 to 10.

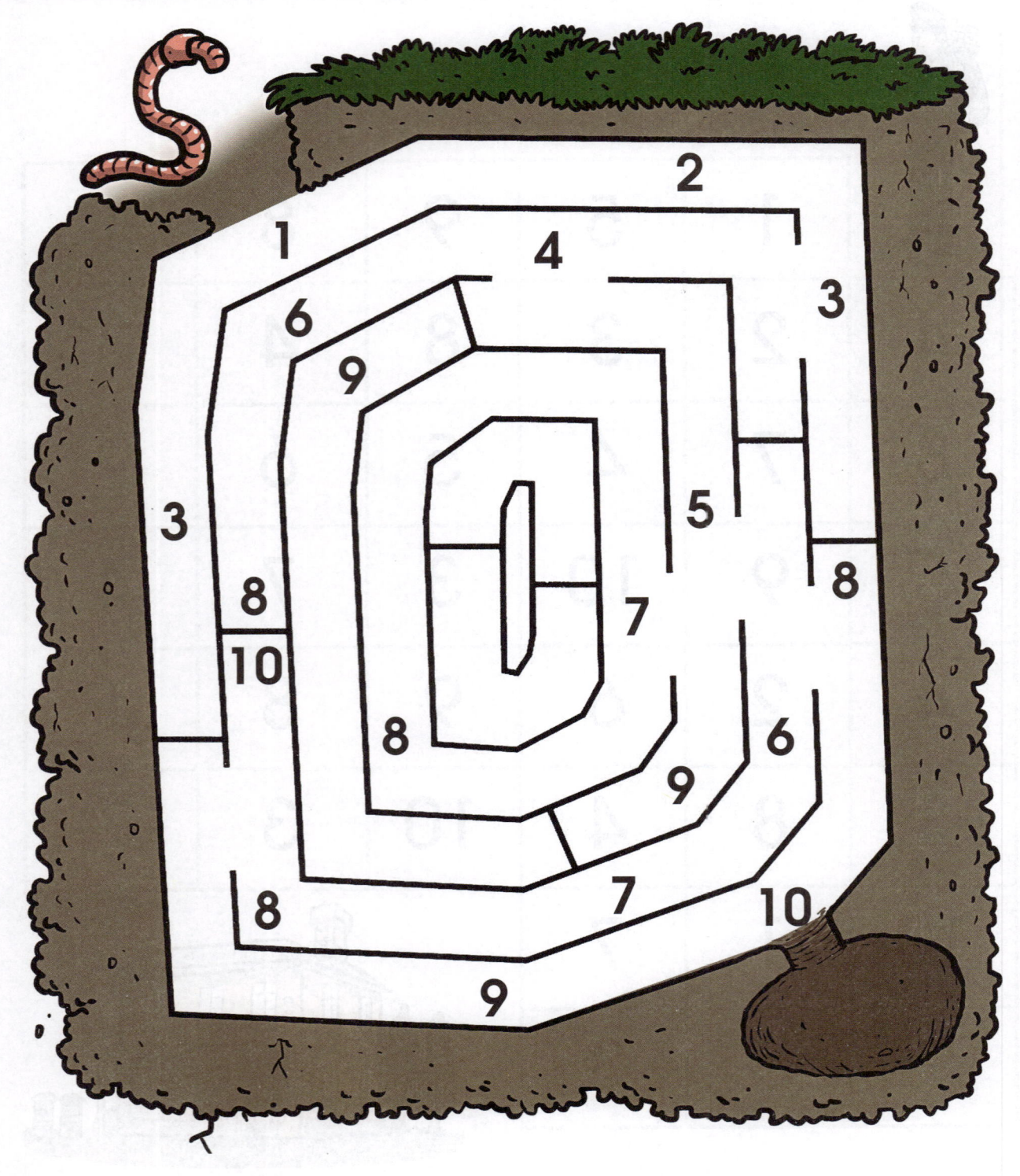

identifying equal groups

Date: _____

Circle the pictures with the same number as in the first picture.

identifying equal groups

Date: _____

Draw a line to match groups of equal numbers.

forming equal groups

Date: _____

Color the correct number of flowers to form equal groups.

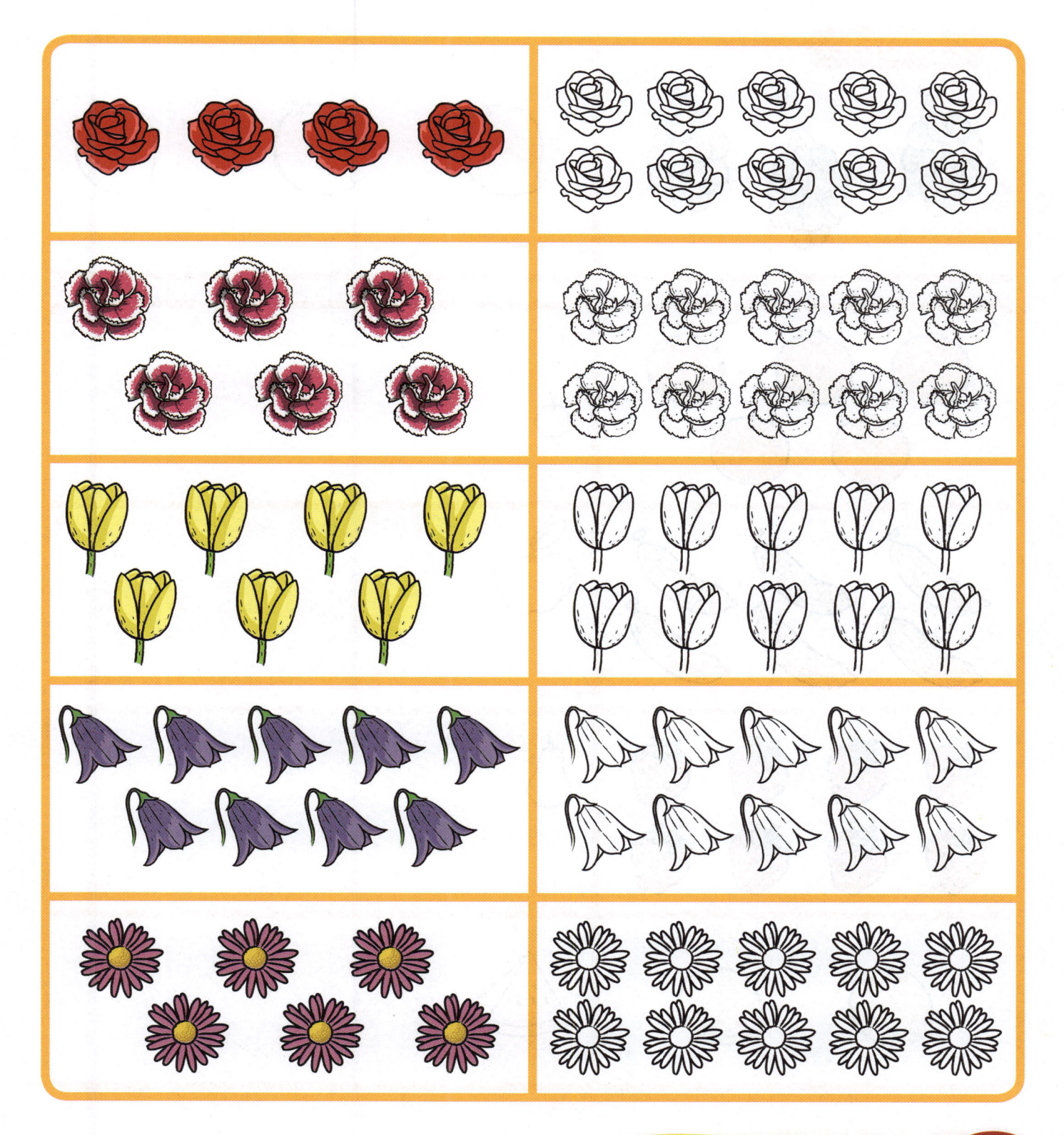

forming equal groups   Date: _____

Draw the correct number of fruits to form equal groups.

counting more than

Date: _____

Circle the picture with more in each box.

1. a) / b)
2. a) / b)
3. a) / b)
4. a) / b)

Numbers 1 to 10 • K1

counting more than

Date: _____

Color the dog with more spots in each picture.

counting more than

Date: _____

Circle the correct number of objects.

Example	
More than 5	(marbles)

More than 3	(shells)

More than 7	(stamps)

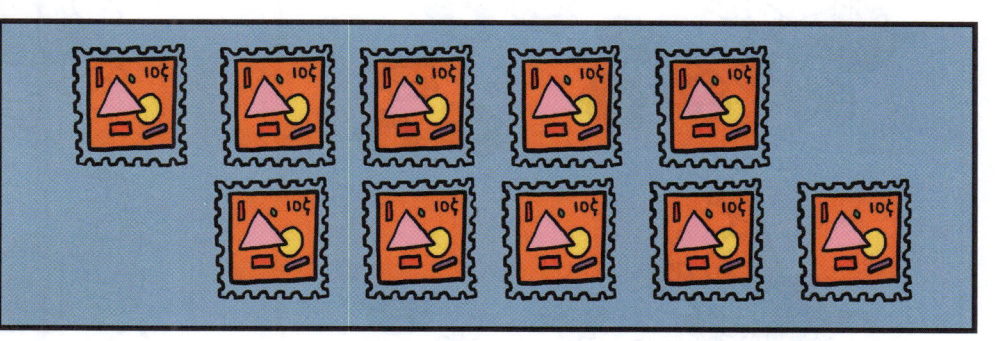

More than 4	(eels)

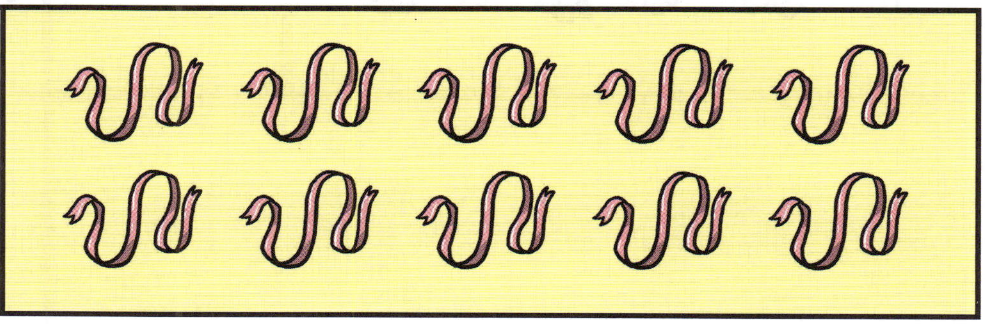

counting less than

Date: _____

Circle the picture with less in each box.

1.
   a)
   b)

2.
   a)
   b)

3.
   a)
   b)

4.
   a)
   b)

counting less than

Date: _____

Color the cat with fewer stripes in each picture.

counting less than

Date: _____

Color the correct number of objects.

Example

Less than 5

Less than 3

Less than 7

Less than 9

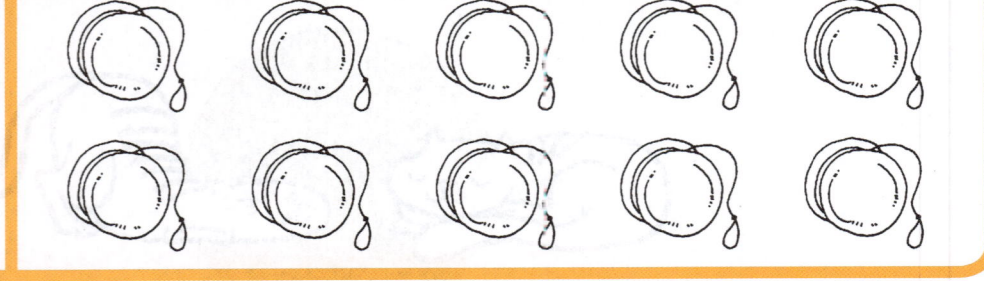

Numbers Practice Test

Fill in the bubble next to the correct answer.

1. Count the number of wells.

   ○ A 1   ○ C 3
   ○ B 2   ○ D 4

2. Count the number of brooms.

   ○ A 1   ○ C 4
   ○ B 3   ○ D 5

Numbers Practice Test

Fill in the bubble next to the correct answer.

3. Count the number of goggles.

○ A 1   ○ C 3
○ B 2   ○ D 4

4. Count the number of forks.

○ A 1   ○ C 4
○ B 3   ○ D 5

Numbers Practice Test

Fill in the bubble next to the correct answer.

5. Count the number of pails.

   ○ A 1
   ○ B 8
   ○ C 9
   ○ D 10

6. Count the number of tortoises.

   ○ A 5
   ○ B 6
   ○ C 7
   ○ D 8

Numbers Practice Test

Fill in the bubble next to the correct answer.

7. Count the number of bells.

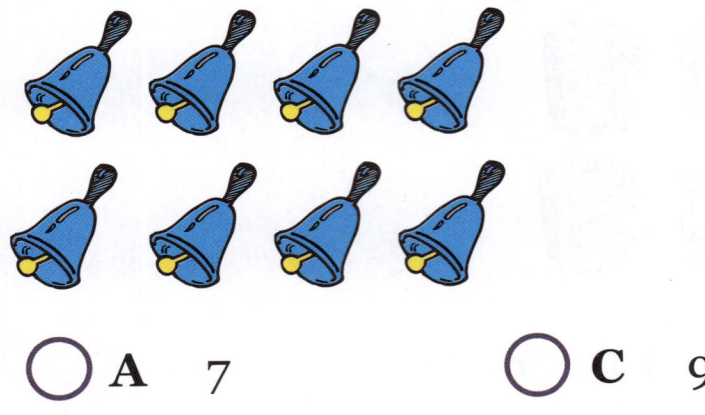

- A 7
- B 8
- C 9
- D 10

8. Count the number of light bulbs.

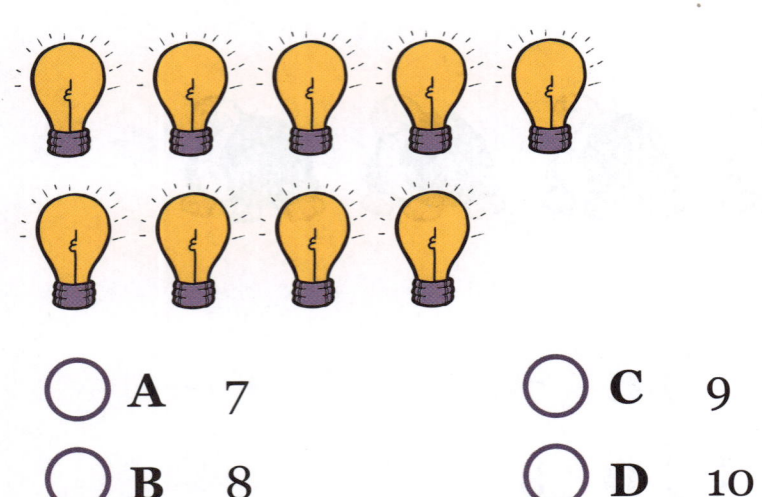

- A 7
- B 8
- C 9
- D 10

Numbers Practice Test

Fill in the bubble next to the correct answer.

9. Count the number of whales.

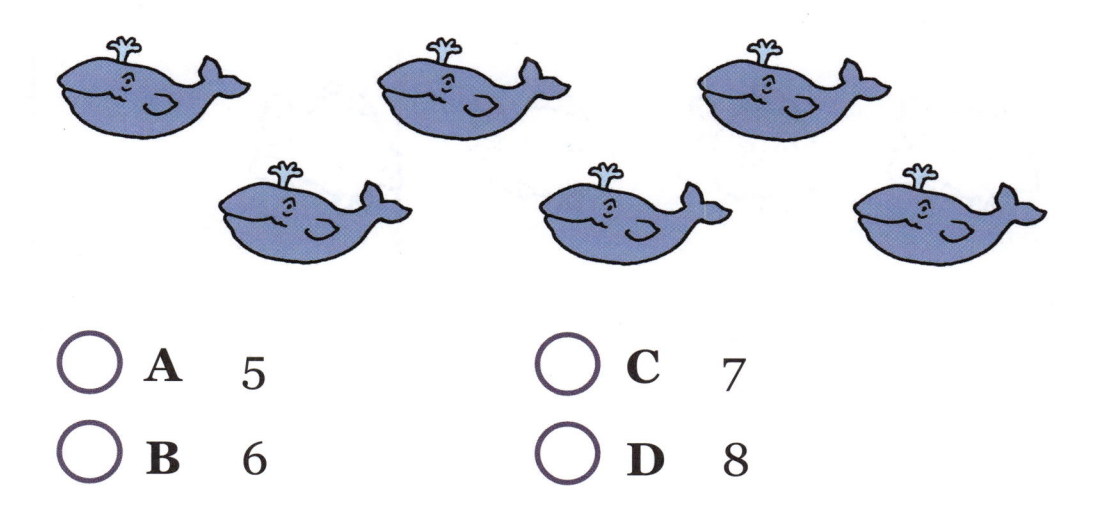

- A 5
- B 6
- C 7
- D 8

10. Count the number of starfish.

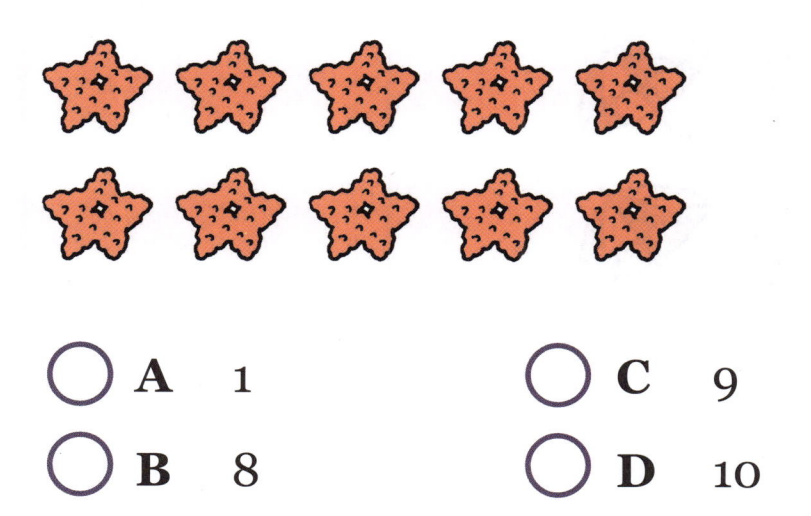

- A 1
- B 8
- C 9
- D 10

Numbers 1 to 10 • K1   75

Numbers Practice Test

Fill in the bubble next to the correct answer.

11. Count the number of fish.

- A   5
- B   6
- C   less than 5
- D   more than 5

12. Count the number of umbrellas.

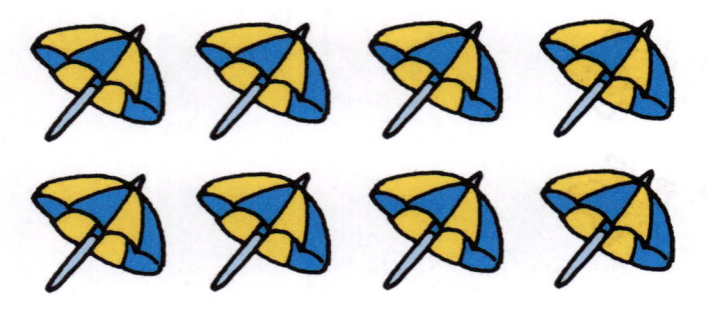

- A   6
- B   10
- C   less than 10
- D   more than 8

Answer Key

Page 6-37

Review that numbers and words have been formed correctly and directions have been followed.

Page 38

2 horses, 3 goats, 4 sheep, 2 cows

Page 39

7 cylinders, 7 cubes, 4 pyramids, 3 L-shaped blocks

Page 40

8 oranges, 10 apples, 2 watermelons, 6 bananas

Page 41-48

Review that directions have been followed.

Page 49

Review that directions have been followed and the right number is written. 6.

Page 50-55

Review that directions have been followed.

Page 56

7, 4, 4, 8

Page 57

3, 5, 6, 9
Review that the dots are joined in the right order.

Page 58-64, 66-67

Review that directions have been followed.

Page 65

| 1. b | 2. a | 3. a | 4. b |

Page 68

| 1. a | 2. a | 3. b | 4. a |

Page 69-70

Review that directions have been followed.

Page 71-76

1. D	2. B	3. B	4. D
5. D	6. B	7. B	8. C
9. B	10. D	11. A	12. C

Scholastic Learning Express

Congratulations!

I, _____,

am a Scholastic Superstar!

I have completed Numbers 1 to 10 K1.

Paste a photo or draw a picture of yourself.

Presented on _____

For page 7

For page 10

For page 13

For page 16

For page 19

For page 22

For page 25

For page 28

For page 31

For page 34

Great!
Well Done!
Good Job
Terrific
Keep It Up!
Super Star!
YOU DID IT!
Keep It Up!
AWESOME
Fantastic!
Keep It Up!
YOU DID IT!
Super Star!
Terrific
Well Done!
Great!
Keep It Up!
Super Star!
YOU DID IT!
Keep It Up!